# WORD POWER

## 100 Words Every 4th GRADER Should Know

New York • Toronto • London • Auckland • Sydney
Mexico City • New Delhi • Hong Kong • Buenos Aires

Impress your friends!

Excel in School!

# AMAZING
# WORD
# POWER

Ace the tests!

Delight your parents!

## Welcome to Amazing Word Power!

By picking up this book you've entered the world of Amazing Words. And you're on your way to building your own Amazing Word Power.

There are 100 great words in this book. Some you may know already. Some may look familiar. But many of them are meant to challenge you! The illustrations and easy-to-understand definitions will help you to learn and remember them.

Ready? Before you get started, you may want to do the following:

1. Use the Checklist that starts on page 125 along with the back cover flap to see what words you know and don't know. (Be sure to use a dry-erase marker.) Do this again in a couple of weeks. This will help you keep track of your growing word power.

2. Check out the Word Power Tips on page 124. Following these tips will help you boost your word learning.

3. Learn more about the words. Many words have several definitions. We didn't include all these definitions, but you can find them—as well as information about the origins of the words—by looking in a dictionary or searching in an online dictionary.

4. Have fun!

# Contents

# 1

# tepid

(tep-id) adjective

## What It Means

Just slightly warm

## How to Use It

Sophia's cocoa was *tepid* by the time she drank it.

## More About It

*I'm hot for hot dogs. I'm tepid for tacos.*

**⊜ Synonym** lukewarm

Tepid ~~Hot~~ Lunches

# sweltering

(**swel**-tur-ing) adjective

## What It Means

Very hot

## How to Use It

The beach is crowded during *sweltering* weather.

## More About It

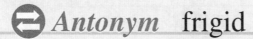 *Antonym*   frigid

 Ah! It's sweltering! I'm melting!

# 3

# balmy

(**bah**-mee) adjective

## What It Means

Pleasantly warm weather

## How to Use It

The island weather was so *balmy* that we never needed jackets.

## More About It

**= *Synonym*** mild

I like to play ball when it's balmy outside. I call it Balmy Ball!

# brisk

(brisk) adjective

## What It Means
Cold and energizing

## How to Use It
The *brisk* weather was perfect for hiking.

## More About It
 *Brisk* can also mean active and lively.

Brrr! It's brrrisk!

# humid

(**hyoo**-mid) adjective

*My mom has big hair when it is humid!*

## What It Means

Damp and moist

## How to Use It

The *humid* weather helped the plants stay green.

## More About It

**= Synonym**   muggy

# Activity Sheet

**Who's who? Draw a line to match the names to the correct pictures.**

1. **Sweltering Sam**

A.

2. **Brisk Bonnie**

B.

3. **Balmy Ben**

C.

4. **Humid Harry**

D.

5. **Tepid Tina**

E.

**Now put everyone in order, from coldest to hottest.**

1. _____

2. _____

3. _____

4. _____

5. _____

# thrifty

(**thrif-tee**) adjective

## What It Means

Careful about wasting money, food, or supplies

## How to Use It

*Thrifty* shoppers are always looking for bargains.

## More About It

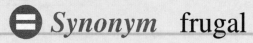 **=** *Synonym*　frugal

TUNA ON SALE!!!

Being _thrifty_ is nifty. I don't spend, but I lend.

# negotiate

(ni-**goh**-shee-ate) verb

## What It Means

To bargain or discuss something so that you can come to an agreement

*Kids unite! Negotiate later bedtimes! (unless you're too tired...)*

## How to Use It

Ella *negotiated* a good price for the baseball cap.

## More About It

◀▶ *Related word* negotiation

Can we negotiate?

# warranty

(**wor**-uhn-*tee*) noun

I ♥ u 4ever. (That's a lifetime warranty!)

## What It Means

A guarantee

## How to Use It

The video-game player came with a two-year *warranty*.

## More About It

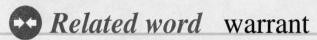 *Related word*   warrant

# redeem

(ri-**deem**) verb

## What It Means

To exchange something for
money or merchandise

*My mom always redeems coupons.*

## How to Use It

Charlie *redeemed* the coupon
for a new video game.

## More About It

◄►► *Related word* redemption

Coupon
Redeem
$5.00

# 10

# rebate

(**ree**-bayt) noun

### What It Means

A refund you receive for part of the money you paid for something

### How to Use It

Charlie got a $5 *rebate* on his video game.

### More About It

*rebate* can also be used as a verb.

A $15 rebate on a $14 item? Now that's a good deal!

# Activity Sheet

Use the clues to complete the puzzle.

**ACROSS**

1. A guarantee

5. To bargain or to discuss something so that you can come to an agreement

**DOWN**

2. To be careful about spending money

3. To exchange something for money or merchandise

4. A refund you receive for part of the money you paid for something

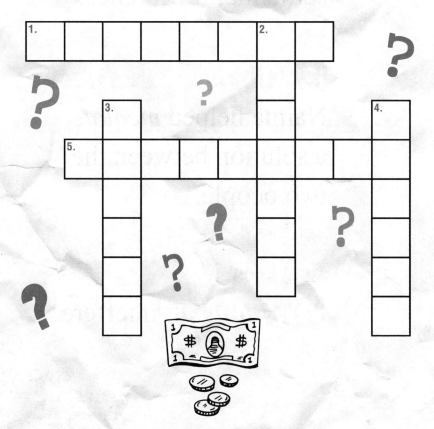

# 11

# mediate

(**mee**-dee-*ate*) verb

## What It Means

To help two people or groups settle their differences

## How to Use It

Naima helped *mediate* a solution between the two people.

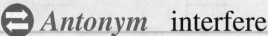

I want chocolate. My brother wants vanilla. who will mediate?

## More About It

⇄ *Antonym*   interfere

# mediocre

(**mee**-dee-**oh**-kur) adjective

## What It Means

Neither good nor bad; ordinary

*My violin playing isn't mediocre. It's extraordinary!*

## How to Use It

The *mediocre* movie didn't attract a large audience.

## More About It

➡️ *Related word*   mediocrity

Blah. This oatmeal is mediocre.

# 13 medieval

(mee-**dee**-vuhl) adjective

*Oh, I get it. Med means middle or between.*

## What It Means

Having to do with the Middle Ages

## How to Use It

Josie spent two hours in the *medieval* exhibit at the museum.

## More About It

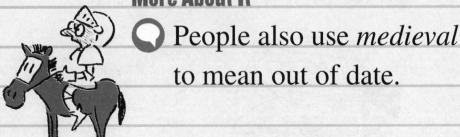 People also use *medieval* to mean out of date.

# media

(**mee-dee-uh**) noun

*TV and the Internet are my favorite media.*

## What It Means

Means for communicating information to many people; radio, TV, and newspapers are examples of media

## How to Use It

We rely on the *media* to report the news fairly.

## More About It

The singular of *media* is *medium*.

# 15

# intermediate

(*in*-tur-**mee**-dee-*it*) adjective

*Intermediate is not for beginners!*

## What It Means

In between two things

## How to Use It

Since Alyssa had played piano for two years, she was ready for an *intermediate* class.

INTERMEDIATE

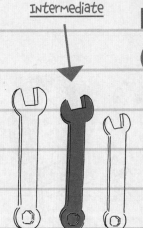

## More About It

🔵 *Synonym*  middle

# Activity Sheet

**What word can help you remember the meaning of the Latin root *med*? Use the clues to fill in the correct words below. Then, write the boxed letters at the bottom of the page.**

1. Something that is between two things
2. Having to do with the Middle Ages
3. Really ordinary
4. A way to communicate to lots of people
5. Another name for the medieval time period
6. When you _____, you help two people come to an agreement.

1. _ _ _ _ _ □ _ _ _ _ _

2. _ _ _ □ _ _ _ _ _

3. _ _ □ _ _ _ _ _

4. _ _ □ _ _ _

*I'm in between.*

5. _ _ _ _ □ _ _ _ _

6. _ □ _ _ _ _ _

When you see the Latin Root *med*,
think of something in the _ _ _ _ _ _ .
1   2   3   4   5   6

# ebullient

(i-**bool**-yint) adjective

## What It Means

Lively and full
of enthusiasm

## How to Use It

Dominic was the most
*ebullient* student in his class.

## More About It

**=** *Synonym*   enthusiastic

Yippee! Hooray! Fantastic! Terrific! I'm ebullient today!

# arrogant

(**a**-ruh-guhnt) adjective

## What It Means

Conceited or too proud

*I'm not <u>arrogant</u>. I'm just better than you. Just kidding...*

## How to Use It

After winning just one game, Jasmine became very *arrogant*.

## More About It

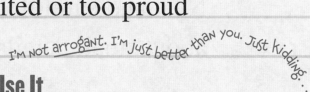 *Antonym* humble

Look how handsome I am!

# 18

# meticulous

(muh-**tik**-yuh-luhss) adjective

### What It Means

Neat and careful about small details

### How to Use It

Lara was *meticulous* about organizing her desk.

### More About It

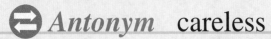 *Antonym* careless

*you have to be meticulous about spelling "meticulous."*

# impetuous

(im-**pech**-oo-uhss) adjective

## What It Means

Acting suddenly,
without thinking first

## How to Use It

Quitting the swim team
was an *impetuous* decision.

## More About It

**＝** *Synonym*  hasty

For me, joining the swim team was an impetuous decision!

# presumptuous

(pri-**zuhm**-choo-uhss) adjective

## What It Means

Tending to believe something is true without checking that you have all the facts

## How to Use It

It was *presumptuous* of Aidan to eat all the ice cream.

## More About It

 *Related word*   presume

*Of course, I did my homework. Don't be presumptuous!*

# Activity Sheet

**How would your friends describe you? Answer the questions and follow the arrows to find out! Some of the words come from earlier sections of this book.**

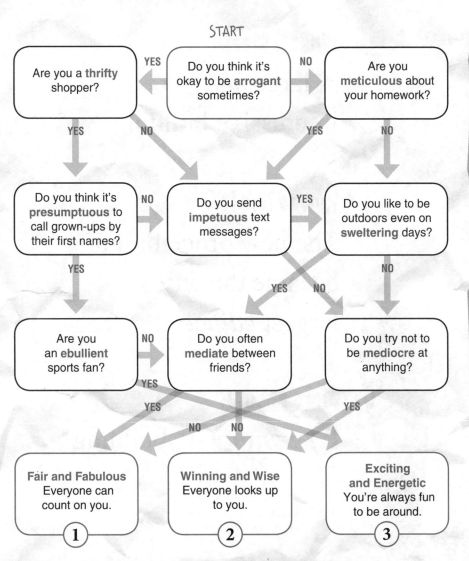

START

Are you a **thrifty** shopper?

YES

Do you think it's okay to be **arrogant** sometimes?

NO

Are you **meticulous** about your homework?

YES    NO    YES    NO

Do you think it's **presumptuous** to call grown-ups by their first names?

NO

Do you send **impetuous** text messages?

YES

Do you like to be outdoors even on **sweltering** days?

YES    NO

Are you an **ebullient** sports fan?

NO

Do you often **mediate** between friends?

Do you try not to be **mediocre** at anything?

YES    YES    NO    YES

NO    NO

**Fair and Fabulous**
Everyone can count on you.

1

**Winning and Wise**
Everyone looks up to you.

2

**Exciting and Energetic**
You're always fun to be around.

3

# edifice

(**ed**-uh-fiss) noun

## What It Means

A large and impressive building

## How to Use It

The new office building became the city's largest *edifice*.

## More About It

⊜ *Synonym*   building

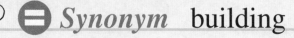

*The Empire State Building is my favorite edifice.*

# turret

(**tur**-it) noun

## What It Means

A small narrow tower

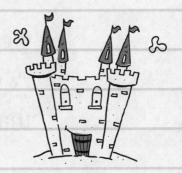

## How to Use It

The castle had a *turret* at each of its four corners.

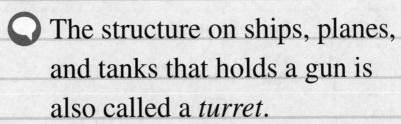

Ahoy! Climb to the turret. I see a ship coming.

## More About It

The structure on ships, planes, and tanks that holds a gun is also called a *turret*.

# spire

(**spire**) noun

### What It Means

A structure on a building that comes to a point

### How to Use It

The church's *spire* reached 80 feet into the air.

### More About It

💬 *Spire* comes from a German word meaning "spear."

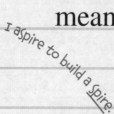

I aspire to build a spire.

# facade

(fuh-**sahd**) noun

## What It Means

The front part
of a building; a
fake front

My house has an aluminum facade.

## How to Use It

The *facade* of our
school is made of brick.

## More About It

*Facade* comes from
an old French word
meaning "face."

# plaza

(plaz-uh) noun

*No skateboarding in the plaza? Darn!*

## What It Means

A public square in a town or city

## How to Use It

Our town festivals are always held in the *plaza*.

## More About It

💬 The English language borrowed the word *plaza* from Spanish.

# Activity Sheet

**Use the clues to complete the puzzle.**

**ACROSS**

1. A bird is sitting on the church's _____.

5. There are four columns on the _____ of the Town Hall.

**DOWN**

2. Public square in a town or city

3. A synonym for *building*

4. The school has a _____ on top of it.

# palatable

(**pal**-i-*tuh*-buhl) adjective

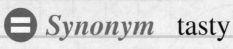

My pizza is palatable but tepid. I need to reheat it.

## What It Means

Agreeable or pleasant-tasting.

## How to Use It

Squirrels find nuts very *palatable*.

## More About It

⊜ *Synonym*   tasty

# inedible

(in-**ed**-uh-buhl) adjective

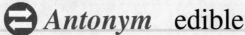
*If dog food is inedible, then why does Ruffles eat it?*

## What It Means

Not fit to be eaten

## How to Use It

The food on the plane was *inedible*.

## More About It

 *Antonym*   edible

**28**

# culinary

(**kuh**-luh-ner-ee) adjective

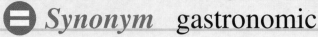

*My culinary skills are mediocre.*

## What It Means

Anything having to do with cooking

## How to Use It

My father has great *culinary* skills.

## More About It

⊜ *Synonym*   gastronomic

"Bon appetit!"

# delectable

(duh-**lek**-tuh-buhl) adjective

## What It Means

Very delicious

## How to Use It

The ice cream at the party was truly *delectable*.

## More About It

⊜ *Synonym*   yummy

I hereby decree that these desserts are delectable.

# 30

# savory

(**say-vuh-ree**) adjective

## What It Means

Pleasing to the taste or smell

## How to Use It

Ana couldn't wait to taste all the *savory* foods on the table.

*Savory soup provides satisfying sustenance.*

## More About It

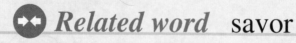 *Related word*  savor

# Activity Sheet

What delectable fruits always travel in groups of two? To find the answer to this riddle, color in any space that contains two words that are synonyms. Some of the words are from earlier sections of this book.

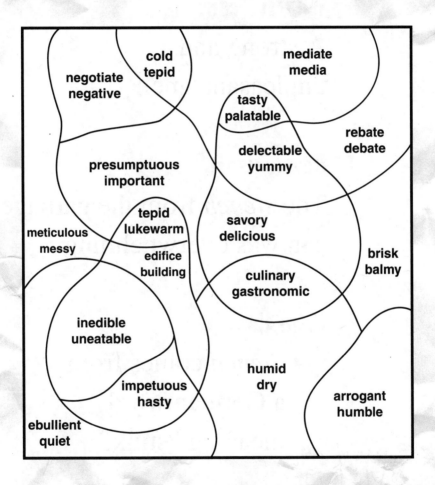

# stench

(stench) noun

## What It Means

A strong and unpleasant smell

## How to Use It

The *stench* from the garbage can was overwhelming.

## More About It

*Stench* comes from a German word meaning "stink."

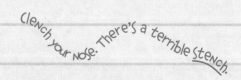

Clench your nose. There's a terrible stench.

# putrid

(**pyoo**-trid) adjective

## What It Means

Rotten and smelly

## How to Use It

The fish left on the dock filled the air with a *putrid* odor.

## More About It

*Putrid* comes from the Latin word that means "to rot."

Ew! Gross. I found the sandwich I dropped in the car last week. Now it's *putrid*.

DO NOT CROSS   DO N

# rancid

(**ran**-sid) adjective

## What It Means

Spoiled or gone bad

## How to Use It

The chicken gave off a *rancid* smell.

## More About It

 ***Related word*** rancidness

Note to Self: Stay away from refrigerator—Rancid cheese inside.

# fragrance

(**fray**-gruhnss) noun

## What It Means

A pleasing smell

## How to Use It

The *fragrance* of the baking cookies filled the house.

## More About It

 *Related word* fragrant

I love the fragrance of flowers.

# 35

# aromatic

(a-roh-**ma**-tik) adjective

## What It Means

Having a very
pleasant smell

## How to Use It

The *aromatic* candle filled
the air with a sweet smell.

## More About It

↔ *Related word*   aroma

Mom overdoes the candle thing: way too aromatic in here.

# Activity Sheet

**What always smells, but has no odor? Write the correct word for each clue. Then write the boxed letters on the lines at the bottom of the page to answer the riddle.**

1. Spoiled or gone bad
2. A pleasing smell, like cookies baking
3. Pleasant smelling, like a pine tree
4. Stink
5. Putrid means smelly and _____

1. __ □ __ __ __ __

2. __ __ __ __ __ □ __ __

3. __ __ □ __ __ __ __ __

4. □ __ __ __ __ __

5. __ __ __ □ __

__ __ __ __ __    always smells, but has no odor.
1   2   3   4   5

# fracture

(frak-chur) verb

## What It Means

To break or crack something, especially a bone

## How to Use It

The X-ray showed that Adam had *fractured* his arm.

## More About It

*Fracture* can also be used as a noun.

Ow! I think I *fractured* my finger in the fridge door!

# fragment

(**frag**-muhnt) noun

*My dog ate my homework, but I managed to save a fragment.*

## What It Means

A small piece or a part that is broken off

## How to Use It

When the dish fell, it broke into *fragments*.

## More About It

💬 *Fragment* can also be used as a verb.

# 38

# fragile

(**fraj**-il) adjective

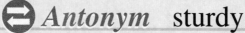 *Don't tease me. My feelings are fragile.*

## What It Means

Delicate or easily broken

## How to Use It

Rebecca carefully placed the *fragile* vase in the box.

## More About It

⇄ *Antonym*   sturdy

# infraction

(in-**frak**-shuhn) noun

*Passing notes in class is a minor infraction, right?*

## What It Means

An action that breaks a rule or law

## How to Use It

Any *infraction* of the rules means detention.

## More About It

= *Synonym* violation

# infringe

(in-**frinj**) verb

Keep out. Don't infringe on my privacy.

## What It Means

To overstep a boundary or do something that affects someone else's rights

## How to Use It

The loud noise at the party *infringed* on the neighbors' right to peace and quiet.

## More About It

⊜ *Synonym* trespass

# Activity Sheet

**What is so fragile, that even saying its name can break it? Write the correct word for each clue. Then write the boxed letters on the lines at the bottom of the page to answer the riddle.**

1. An antonym for *fragile*
2. To overstep a boundary
3. Easily broken
4. A small, broken off piece of something

5. An action that breaks a rule or law
6. To break or crack something
7. A synonym for *fracture*

1. ☐ _ _ _ _ _

2. _ _ _ _ ☐ _ _ _

3. _ _ _ _ ☐ _

4. _ _ _ _ ☐ _ _

5. _ ☐ _ _ _ _ _

6. _ _ ☐ _ _ _

7. _ _ ☐ _ _

_ _ _ _ _ _ _
1 2 3 4 5 6 7

# 41 banter

(**ban**-tur) verb

### What It Means

To tease someone
in a friendly way

### How to Use It

My brother likes
to *banter* with me.

### More About It

💬 *Banter* can also
be a noun.

yes, you are. No, I'm not. Yes, you are. No, I'm not. Are we bantering?

# indulge

(in-**duhlj**) verb

## What It Means

To give in to something

## How to Use It

Nick's mother always *indulges* his sweet tooth.

## More About It

 *Related word* indulgent

Yum! I'd like to indulge in some delectable pie right now.

Ready to indulge?

# 43

# relish

(**rel**-ish) verb

## What It Means

To enjoy something greatly

## How to Use It

I *relish* my free
time on weekends.

## More About It

💬 *Relish* can also be
used as a noun.

*Ketchup, mustard, mayonnaise, relish: I relish them all!*

# revel

(**rev**-uhl) verb

## What It Means

To take great satisfaction in something

## How to Use It

Seong *reveled* in his new role as the band's drummer.

## More About It

⊜ *Synonym*   enjoy

Shockingly, I would <u>revel</u> in a week with no school!

# excursion

(ek-**skur**-zhuhn) noun

## What It Means

A short journey, often to a place of interest

## How to Use It

My grandfather took us on an *excursion*.

## More About It

⊜ *Synonym*   outing

Yippee! A class excursion to the aquarium! I'm ebullient!

# Activity Sheet

**What's your favorite thing to do on a Saturday morning? Keep choosing between pairs to find out! Write your choice for each pair in the box to the right until you get to the last box. Some of the words come from earlier sections of this book.**

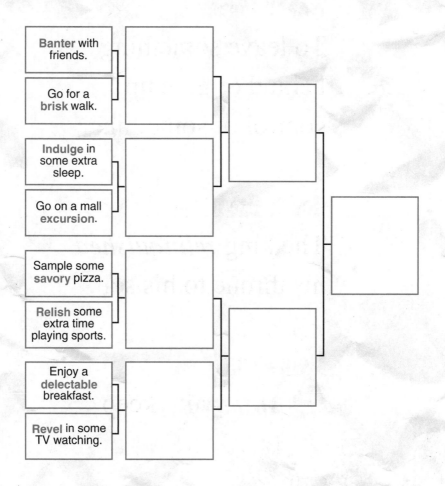

**Banter** with friends.

Go for a **brisk** walk.

**Indulge** in some extra sleep.

Go on a mall **excursion**.

Sample some **savory** pizza.

**Relish** some extra time playing sports.

Enjoy a **delectable** breakfast.

**Revel** in some TV watching.

# 46

# relinquish

(ruh-**ling**-kwish) verb

## What It Means

To leave something behind or give up control of something

## How to Use It

The king *relinquished* his throne to his son.

## More About It

⇄ *Antonym*  keep

*I hereby relinquish the title of messiest person in the house.*

# brawl

(**brawl**) noun

## What It Means

A noisy fight

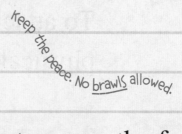

keep the peace. No brawls allowed.

## How to Use It

A *brawl* broke out among the fans watching the football game.

## More About It

= *Synonym*   quarrel

# assail

(uh-**sayl**) verb

## What It Means

To attack violently, either physically or with words

## How to Use It

Being *assailed* by a bully is always scary.

## More About It

**=** *Synonym*   assault

You can't just sail in here and assail me like that!

# dispute

(diss-**pyoot**) verb

Hey, that's my apple. Do you dispute that this is my fruit, you brute?

## What It Means

To say you think someone is wrong about something

## How to Use It

I *disputed* whether my room was clean or not.

## More About It

= *Synonym*   argue

It's mine.

It's mine.

# skirmish

(**skur**-mish) noun

## What It Means

A minor fight

## How to Use It

The *skirmish* for control of the football ended quickly.

## More About It

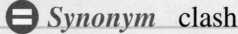 *Synonym*   clash

war > battle > riot > brawl > fight > skirmish

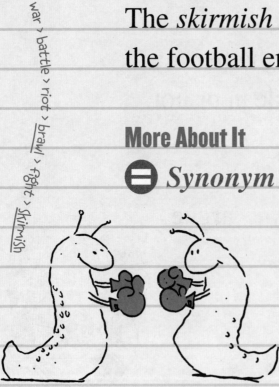

# Activity Sheet

Ready for a boxing match? Draw a line from a glove in the left column to the glove in the right column with the correct definition.

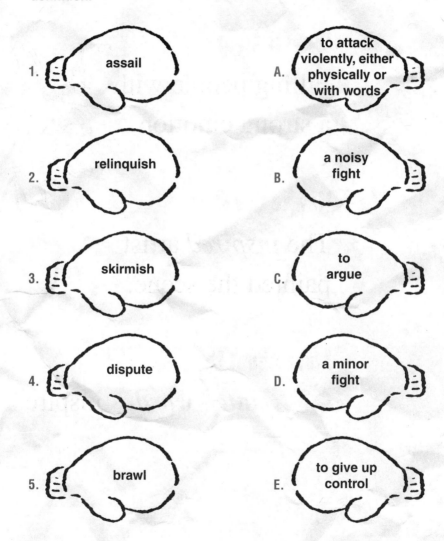

1. assail

A. to attack violently, either physically or with words

2. relinquish

B. a noisy fight

3. skirmish

C. to argue

4. dispute

D. a minor fight

5. brawl

E. to give up control

# 51

# inspired

(in-**spye**-urd) adjective

## What It Means

Filling people with a strong emotion

## How to Use It

The *inspired* artist painted the scene.

## More About It

→ *Related words*   inspire

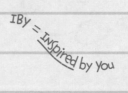

IBY = Inspired by you

# insipid

(in-**sip**-id) adjective

## What It Means

Dull or flat

## How to Use It

The *insipid* play put everyone to sleep.

## More About It

⊜ *Synonym*   boring

*My favorite put-down: This is insipid!*

# intriguing

(in-**treeg**-ing) adjective

*Dad is making a culinary surprise in the kitchen. Intriguing.*

## What It Means

Exciting and engaging

## How to Use It

I found the book's title *intriguing*.

## More About It

**= Synonym**   interesting

# provocative

(pruh-**vok**-uh-tiv) adjective

## What It Means

Intended to get a
reaction from people

## How to Use It

The *provocative* magazine headline
made me want to read it.

## More About It

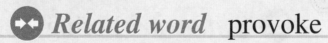 *Related word* provoke

Title of <u>provocative</u> book I'd like to write: Sleeping makes you smarter.

# tedious

(**tee-dee-uhss**) adjective

## What It Means

Boring and unchanging

## How to Use It

Nina found it *tedious* to have to fill out so many forms.

## More About It

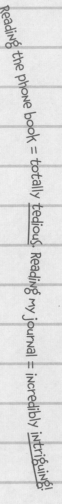

= *Synonym*   boring

Reading the phone book = totally tedious. Reading my journal = incredibly intriguing!

# Activity Sheet

**The critics have written their movie reviews. But they need some help with the headlines. Read each movie description. Then circle the headline that best fits it.**

1. This movie will make you want to change your life.

   Ⓐ An Inspired Must-See!          Ⓑ A Tedious Must-See!

2. The boring characters and plodding plot in this movie will leave you wishing you'd stayed home and watched TV.

   Ⓐ What an Insipid Movie!         Ⓑ What a Provocative Movie!

3. Seeing the same prank over and over in this movie will put you to sleep.

   Ⓐ Year's Most Intriguing Film    Ⓑ Year's Most Tedious Film

4. You'll be talking to friends about this movie for weeks!

   Ⓐ Provocative & Powerful         Ⓑ Insipid & Powerful

5. This mystery will keep you guessing long after you leave the theater.

   Ⓐ What an Insipid Movie!         Ⓑ What an Intriguing Movie!

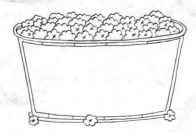

# 56

# suspend

(suh-**spend**) verb

*waiting for my report card is like time suspended.*

## What It Means

To hang something. It also means to delay or stop something from happening.

## How to Use It

The sloth *suspended* itself from a tree branch.

## More About It

 *Related word*   suspense

# depend

(di-**pend**) verb

## What It Means

To need or rely on
something or someone

## How to Use It

The ducklings *depend*
on their mother.

## More About It

⊜ *Synonym*   need

I depend on my mom, too!

# pendant

(**pen**-duhnt) noun

*My grandmother's pendant has a picture in it.*

## What It Means

A hanging ornament, especially one on a necklace.

## How to Use It

The ruby *pendant* around her neck caught everyone's attention.

## More About It

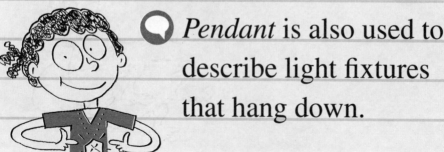 *Pendant* is also used to describe light fixtures that hang down.

# append

(uh-**pend**) verb

## What It Means

To add a part
on to something

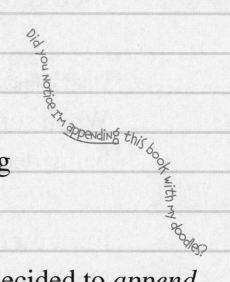

*Did you notice I'm appending this book with my doodles?*

## How to Use It

The principal decided to *append* the newsletter with a chart.

## More About It

**⊷ *Related word*** appendix

# pending

(**pen**-ding) adjective

## What It Means

When something is still being decided upon

## How to Use It

Our class poll results are still *pending*.

## More About It

**>< Related word** impending

The patent for my new invention is still pending.

# Activity Sheet

**Use the clues to complete the puzzle. Some of the words come from earlier sections of this book.**

### ACROSS

2. A word that means boring and unchanging
6. To add a part on to something
7. To need something to survive

### DOWN

1. When something is still being decided upon
3. Minor fights or clashes
4. The blizzard caused train service to be _____.
5. An ornament on a chain that you wear around your neck

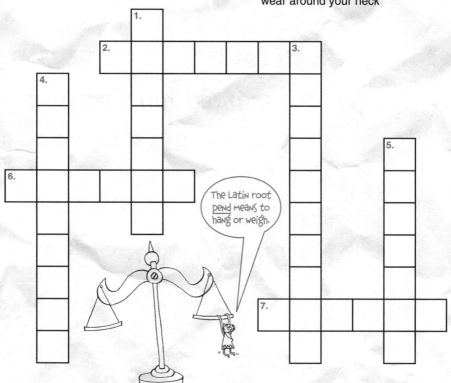

# taunt

(**tawnt**) verb

Please don't *taunt* the turtles. They get terribly traumatized.

### What It Means

To try to upset someone
by teasing him or her

### How to Use It

Alex *taunted* June because
she didn't run fast in the race.

### More About It

💬 *Taunt* can also
be a noun.

# disdain

**(dis-dayn)** verb

*I disdain spiders. They're creepy!*

## What It Means

To dislike something or someone and look down on it or them

## How to Use It

My dog *disdains* my cat.

## More About It

⇌ *Antonym*   admire

You know I disdain you.

Well, I've always admired you.

Love It/Hate It

# laud

(lawd) verb

## What It Means

To praise someone

## How to Use It

Everyone *lauded* Eduardo
for his high score.

## More About It

▶◀ *Related word*  laudable

*My dad lauded me for cleaning the garage.*

# acclaim

(uh-**klaym**) noun

*I sure could use some acclaim.*

## What It Means

Enthusiastic approval

## How to Use It

The actor was used to receiving *acclaim* from his fans.

## More About It

*Acclaim* can also be used as a verb.

# esteem

(ess-**teem**) noun

I have a lot of esteem for firefighters.

## What It Means

Respect and admiration

## How to Use It

The team held the coach in high *esteem*.

## More About It

◄► *Related word*   esteemed

# Activity Sheet

**Read each clue. Then write the answers in the spiral puzzle. The first one is done for you.**

1. A synonym for *tease*
2. To look down on someone
3. To praise
4. Enthusiastic approval
5. I have great respect and _____ for my father.
6. A synonym for *laud*
7. A synonym for *disdain*
8. If you have esteem for someone, you _____ them.

| | | | | | | 3. |
|---|---|---|---|---|---|---|
| 2. | | 6. | | | | |
| T | | 8. | | | | |
| N | | | ♥ | | | |
| U | | | | | 7. | 4. |
| A | | | | | | |
| 1. T | 5. | | | | | |

START

# tarnish

(**tar**-nish) verb

## What It Means

To become duller
and less bright

## How to Use It

After sitting in the closet
for many years, the silver
became *tarnished*.

## More About It

 *Synonym*   dull

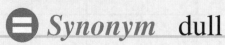

Hey, tell the truth. Don't tarnish my reputation.

# sully

(**suhl**-ee) verb

## What It Means

To make something dirty

## How to Use It

Gina *sullied* her jeans when she fell during recess.

## More About It

**=** *Synonym* soil

Mom gets mad when my dirty shoes sully the floor.

# debris

(duh-**bree**) noun

### What It Means

Pieces of garbage or unwanted material spread about

### How to Use It

*Debris* from the art project covered the classroom floor.

### More About It

 *Synonym*  litter

Let's pick up debris and help keep the beach clean!

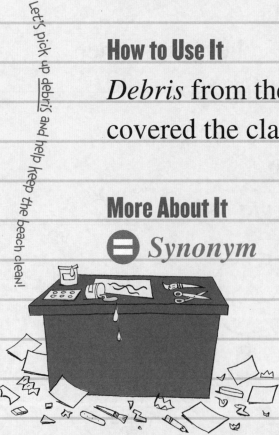

# decrepit

(di-**krep**-it) adjective

## What It Means

Weakened by being
old or overused

## How to Use It

The *decrepit* building looked as
if it were about to fall down.

## More About It

⊜ *Synonym*   shabby

Some people think my jeans are decrepit. I think they're comfortable.

# unkempt

(uhn-**kempt**) adjective

## What It Means

Untidy and messy
in appearance

## How to Use It

The *unkempt* puppy
was in need of a bath.

## More About It

⇄ *Antonym* kempt

You call it unkempt. I call it a hairstyle.

# Activity Sheet

**Time to clean up! Match each broom to the correct dustpan.**

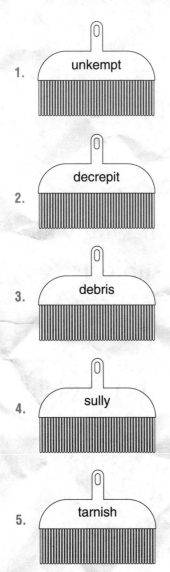

1. unkempt

2. decrepit

3. debris

4. sully

5. tarnish

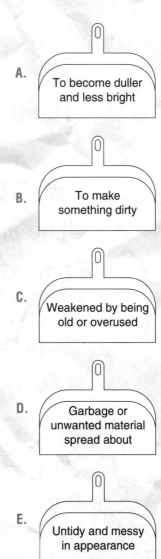

A. To become duller and less bright

B. To make something dirty

C. Weakened by being old or overused

D. Garbage or unwanted material spread about

E. Untidy and messy in appearance

# malevolent

(muh-**lev**-uh-lent) adjective

## What It Means

Hateful or evil

## How to Use It

The *malevolent* king was feared by his subjects.

## More About It

 **⇄** *Antonym*   benevolent

So, the wicked witch was malevolent, right?

# vile

(vile) adjective

## What It Means

Very unpleasant

## How to Use It

Lucas thinks brussels sprouts are *vile*.

## More About It

⊜ *Synonym*   nasty

Movie villains are often <u>vile</u>.

# intrepid

(in-**trep**-id) adjective

## What It Means

Bold and courageous

## How to Use It

The *intrepid* firefighter smashed down the door and rescued the child.

## More About It

⇄ *Antonym*  timid

*when it comes to swimming in the ocean, my dad is intrepid.*

# valor

(**val**-ur) noun

**What It Means**

Great bravery or courage, especially in battle

**How to Use It**

The soldier received a medal for his *valor*.

**More About It**

= *Synonym* heroism

Shall we display our valor on the basketball court?

# illustrious

(i-**luh**-stree-uhss) adjective

## What It Means

Famous for outstanding achievements

## How to Use It

The *illustrious* inventor received great acclaim.

## More About It

**⊜ *Synonym***   celebrated

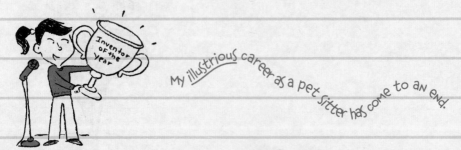

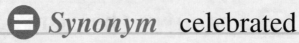

My <u>illustrious</u> career as a pet sitter has come to an end.

# Activity Sheet

**Play the game of Out and Over. Find a word in Box 1 that does not have the same meaning as the other three words. Move that word to Box 2 by writing it on the blank line. Continue to the next box until you reach Box 8. Then complete the sentence in that box.**

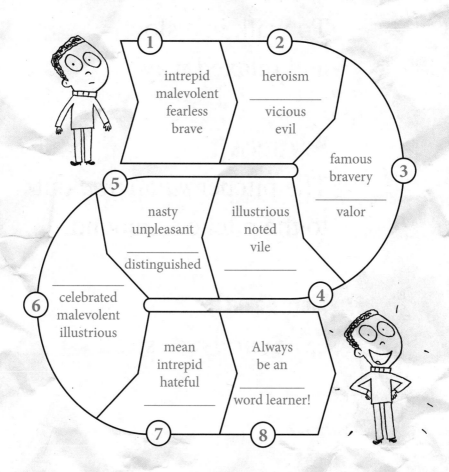

**1**
intrepid
malevolent
fearless
brave

**2**
heroism
_____
vicious
evil

**3**
famous
bravery
_____
valor

**5**
nasty
unpleasant
_____
distinguished

illustrious
noted
vile
_____

**6**
_____
celebrated
malevolent
illustrious

**4**

mean
intrepid
hateful
_____

**8**
Always
be an
_____
word learner!

**7**

# saunter

(**sawn-ter**) verb

*Think I'll saunter into the kitchen for some savory sandwiches.*

### What It Means

To walk in a slow
and relaxed way

### How to Use It

The pitcher *sauntered* out
to the pitcher's mound.

### More About It

≡ *Synonym*   stroll

# stampede

(stam-**peed**) verb

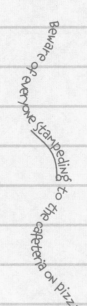

## What It Means

To run in a very fast
and uncontrolled way

## How to Use It

The people in the park
*stampeded* toward their
cars when it started to rain.

## More About It

💬 *Stampede* comes from the
Spanish word *estampida*,
which means "crash."

Beware of everyone stampeding to the cafeteria on pizza day.

# 78

# bound

**(bound)** verb

## What It Means

To move forward quickly, in leaps and jumps

## How to Use It

The dog *bounded* across the room when he heard the doorbell ring.

## More About It

⊜ *Synonym*   leap

*I bound to the door when the pizza is delivered.*

# vault

(**vawlt**) verb

*Let's play leapfrog. I mean, vault-toad.*

## What It Means

To leap over something using your hands to support you

## How to Use It

Liana *vaulted* over the wall to get away from the barking dog.

## More About It

*Vault* is also used to mean a room where things can be safely stored.

# mosey

(**moh**-zee) verb

## What It Means

To walk slowly
or aimlessly

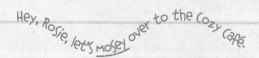

## How to Use It

Mr. Cortez spent an hour
*moseying* through the town.

## More About It

*Mosey* comes from the
Spanish word *vamos*,
which means "let's go."

Hey, Rosie, let's mosey over to the cozy café.

# Activity Sheet

**Use the clues to complete the puzzle.**

**ACROSS**

4. Unhurried hikers often _____ along the park's trail.

6. Cows often _____ when they are scared.

**DOWN**

1. My little brothers _____ down our stairs when the doorbell rings.

2. On Saturdays, I like to _____ around the mall.

3. *Stampede* comes from the Spanish word *estampida* meaning _____.

5. When people stampede, they _____ very quickly.

# serene

(suh-**reen**) adjective

## What It Means

Calm and peaceful

## How to Use It

Jesse enjoys listening to *serene* music.

## More About It

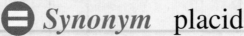 *Synonym* placid

My sister looks serene—when she's sleeping!

# melancholy

(**mel**-uhn-*kol*-ee) adjective

## What It Means

Very sad

## How to Use It

The *melancholy* song made everyone sad.

## More About It

⊜ *Synonym*  unhappy

what makes me melancholy? Being assailed by taunts, insipid TV Shows, and putrid veggies.

# perturbed

(pur-**turbd**) adjective

*Mrs. Paulson was perturbed at us for talking in class.*

## What It Means

To be upset by something or anxious about something

## How to Use It

The class was *perturbed* to hear there would be no recess.

## More About It

⇄ *Antonym*  calm

I'm perturbed by these infractions!

Judge

# irate

(**eye-rate**) adjective

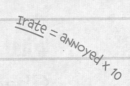

_Irate = annoyed x 10_

## What It Means

Very angry about
something

## How to Use It

Getting a speeding ticket
made my father _irate_.

## More About It

➡ **_Related word_** ire

What do you
mean, "Not palatable?"
I'm irate!

# buoyant

(**boi**-uhnt) adjective

*My "what-makes-me-buoyant" list: moseying in the mall • Sleeping late • Indulging in chocolate cake*

## What It Means

Cheerful and upbeat

## How to Use It

In spite of losing the first race, Jeremy remained *buoyant* about the track meet.

## More About It

➡️ *Related word*   buoy

# Activity Sheet

Play the game of Out and Over. Find a word in Box 1 that does not have the same meaning as the other three words. Move that word to Box 2 by writing it on the blank line. Continue to the next box until you reach Box 8. Then complete the sentence in that box.

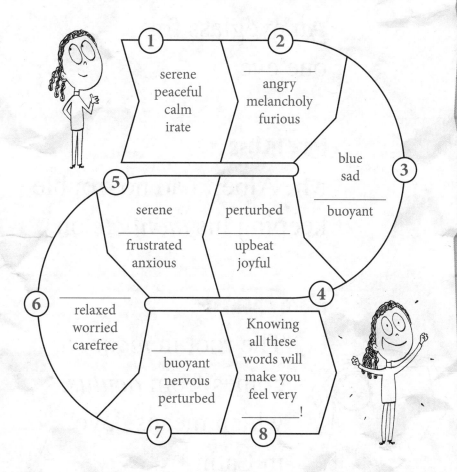

**1**
serene
peaceful
calm
irate

**2**
_____
angry
melancholy
furious

**3**
blue
sad
buoyant

**5**
serene
_____
frustrated
anxious

perturbed
_____
upbeat
joyful

**6**
_____
relaxed
worried
carefree

**4**

buoyant
nervous
perturbed

**8**
Knowing all these words will make you feel very _____!

**7**

# monocle

(**mon**-uh-kuhl) noun

## What It Means

An eyeglass for
one eye

## How to Use It

Mr. Albert had no trouble
keeping his *monocle* on.

## More About It

The root in *monocle*
comes from *oculus*,
which means "eye"
in Latin.

Do two monocles equal a pair?

# monarch

(**mon**-urk) noun

## What It Means

A ruler who reigns over a kingdom or an empire

## How to Use It

Queen Elizabeth has been England's *monarch* since 1952.

## More About It

*Related word*   monarchy

Serene monarch butterflies rule!

# monologue

(**mon**-uh-*log*) noun

### What It Means

A speech given
by one person

### How to Use It

The actor's *monologue* was
the longest in the play.

### More About It

The root in *monologue*
is *logue*, which
means "speak."

Mom has a famous monologue about finishing dinner.

# monotone

(**mon**-uh-tohn) adjective

## What It Means

An unchanging tone of voice, having little expression

## How to Use It

Aubrey's *monotone* speech put everyone to sleep.

## More About It

➡️ *Related word*   monotonous

Oh, I get it. MONO MEANS ONE. MONOTONE = ONE TONE.

# monopoly

(muh-**nop**-uh-lee) noun

*I have a MONOPOLY on Grandpa's affections.*

## What It Means

To have a monopoly on something means to have complete control of it

## How to Use It

Since there was only one store in town, it had a *monopoly* on all sales.

## More About It

⊷ *Related word*   monopolize

# Activity Sheet

**What word can help you remember the meaning of the Greek prefix *mono*? Write the correct word for each clue. Then write the boxed letters on the lines at the bottom of the page.**

1. A ruler of a kingdom or empire
2. A speech given by one person
3. Complete control of something
4. An unchanging tone of voice
5. An eyeglass for one eye

1. ___ ___ ___ [ ] ___ ___ ___

2. ___ ___ [ ] ___ ___ ___ ___

3. ___ ___ [ ] ___ ___ ___ ___

4. ___ ___ [ ] ___ ___ ___ ___

5. ___ ___ ___ ___ [ ]

When you see the Greek prefix *mono* think of something or someone that is

___ ___ ___ ___ ___ .
1   2   3   4   5

# 91

# plausible

(**plaw**-zuh-buhl) adjective

Me as class president = plausible. Me as class clown = likely.

## What It Means

Believable

## How to Use It

The teacher didn't think Tod's excuse was *plausible*.

## More About It

*Related word*   plausibly

After the alien ate my book report...

# droll

(**drohl**) adjective

## What It Means

Amusing, sometimes
in an expected way

## How to Use It

The school assembly speaker
had a *droll* sense of humor.

## More About It

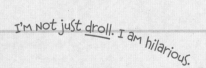 *Synonym*  laughable

I'M NOT JUST <u>droll</u>. I AM hilarious.

# whimsical

(**wim**-zuh-kuhl) adjective

## What It Means

Playful and unpredictable

## How to Use It

The *whimsical* show made us smile.

## More About It

▶◀ *Related word*   whim

I love whimsical books and movies.

# ponder

(**pon-dur**) verb

**When I do puzzles, I ponder for a long, long, long time.**

## What It Means

To think about something very carefully

## How to Use It

I'm *pondering* whether to join the chess club.

## More About It

= *Synonym*   consider

# lampoon

(lam-**poon**) verb

*New Rule: Don't lampoon anyone.*

### What It Means

To make fun of something in a humorous way

### How to Use It

The book *lampoons* silly inventions.

### More About It

⊜ *Synonym*  ridicule

# Activity Sheet

**It's silly riddle time. Complete each silly riddle using one of the words in the box below.**

| | | | | |
|---|---|---|---|---|
| droll | whimsical | lampoon | ponder | plausible |

1. What do you call a troll who's funny?

   _____

2. What does a critical light like to do? _____

4. What do you call buying an icy treat on an impulse?

   _____

3. What did the writer do when she sat by a small lake?

   _____

5. Why did the bull always tell the truth? He was

   _____.

# latter

(lat-ur) noun

## What It Means

The second of two things

## How to Use It

Ignacio played basketball and soccer but preferred the *latter* because it is played outdoors.

## More About It

💬 *Latter* comes from an Old English word meaning "late."

Hmm. Cauliflower or cupcakes? I choose the latter.

-Latter-

# anachronism

(uh-**nak**-ruh-*niz*-uhm) noun

## What It Means

Something that is out
of its proper time

## How to Use It

The big-screen TV seemed like
an *anachronism* in the old castle.

## More About It

 *Related word*   anachronistic

# novel

(**nov-uhl**) adjective

## What It Means

New and unusual

## How to Use It

It's hard to believe that surfing the Internet was once considered *novel*.

## More About It

*Novel* can also be used to mean a book of fiction.

Read a novel aloud? What a novel idea!

# former

(for-mur) noun

Jason and Adrian carpool with us. The *former* lives next door, and Adrian lives two blocks away.

## What It Means

The first of two things that you have been talking about

## How to Use It

If I have a choice between brownies and pie, I always get the *former* because I love chocolate.

## More About It

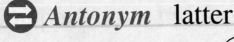 **Antonym** latter

Former

# sequential

(see-**kwen**-shuhl) adjective

Oh no! I guess the steps were sequential. Now my cake is inedible.

## What It Means

Following in a fixed order

## How to Use It

The recipe stressed the importance of completing the steps in *sequential* order.

## More About It

→← *Related word* sequence

Abchedilekj.. Hey, these letters are not sequential. Abcdefghijkl... That's better.

# Activity Sheet

**Read each clue. Then write the answers in the spiral puzzle.**

1. If directions must be followed in a fixed order, they are
   _____.
2. A typewriter is now considered an _____.
3. Something new and unusual is _____.
4. The first of two things you've been talking about.
5. The second of two things you've been talking about.
6. *Former* means the _____ of two things.
7. *Latter* means the _____ of two things.

| | | | | 2. | | |
|---|---|---|---|---|---|---|
| | | | | | 5. | |
| | | | 7. | | | |
| | 4. | | | | | |
| | | | | | | |
| | | | 6. | | | |
| 1. | | | 3. | | | |

START

# Word Power Tips

**Are you ready to add 100 words to your vocabulary? Check out the 10 tips below. They're a great way to help boost your Amazing Word Power!**

1. **Keep Track of Your Progress.** Use the Checklist that starts on page 125 with the back cover flap to keep track of your growing vocabulary. Cover the definitions with the flap and quiz yourself. (Be sure to use a dry-erase marker.) Test yourself every few weeks to see how many new words you have learned.

2. **Say the Word Aloud.** A pronunciation is given for every word, and you'll also find a pronunciation guide on the inside of the back cover flap. Saying the word will help you remember it better. And the more you say it, the better chance you have of remembering it!

3. **Look at the Illustrations.** Some people remember better when they see a picture, so be sure you look at the illustration included for each word. The illustration may be the key to helping you remember the word's meaning.

4. **Read Each Section of the Word Page.** The more times you encounter a word, the more likely you are to remember it. Each page is designed to give you lots of opportunities to see the word and understand how it is used. The More About It sections include additional information about the words (see the key on the inside back cover flap).

5. **Think About the Word Groups.** How are the words in each group related? Do they share a Latin or Greek root? Are they all ways to describe something? If you can remember what group a word is in, it will help you figure out its meaning the next time you see it.

6. **Do the Activity.** At the end of each group of words, there is an activity page. Doing the activity will help you use and remember the words. Plus, they're fun!

7. **Write Your Own Sentence.** It's true: Using a new word in a sentence helps you to remember it.  Try writing your own sentence for each word.

8. **Listen for the Words.** See how often these words come up in conversations, in school, on TV, or in movies.

9. **Look for the Words.** Look for these words online or as you're reading your favorite books or magazines. Make it a game to find them as often as possible.

10. **Use the Words Whenever You Can.** Don't be afraid to exercise your word power! Use your new words as much as you can when you are speaking and writing. You'll amaze your friends, your parents, and your teachers!

1. tepid — tepid: just slightly warm
2. sweltering — sweltering: very hot
3. balmy — balmy: pleasantly warm weather
4. brisk — brisk: cold and energizing
5. humid — humid: damp and moist
6. thrifty — thrifty: careful about not wasting things
7. negotiate — negotiate: to bargain or to discuss something
8. warranty — warranty: a guarantee
9. redeem — redeem: to exchange something for money
10. rebate — rebate: a refund for part of your payment for something
11. mediate — mediate: to help two people agree
12. mediocre — mediocre: ordinary
13. medieval — medieval: having to do with the Middle Ages
14. media — media: means of communication
15. intermediate — intermediate: in between two things
16. ebullient — ebullient: lively and enthusiastic
17. arrogant — arrogant: too proud
18. meticulous — meticulous: carefully attentive to details
19. impetuous — impetuous: acting without thinking first
20. presumptuous — presumptuous: assuming something is true
21. edifice — edifice: a large building
22. turret — turret: a small narrow tower
23. spire — spire: a pointed structure on top of a building
24. facade — facade: the front of a building
25. plaza — plaza: a town square
26. palatable — palatable: pleasant-tasting
27. inedible — inedible: not fit to be eaten
28. culinary — culinary: having to do with cooking
29. delectable — delectable: very delicious
30. savory — savory: pleasing to eat
31. stench — stench: a strong, unpleasant smell
32. putrid — putrid: rotten and smelly
33. rancid — rancid: spoiled or gone bad

(Continued on page 127)

# Answer Key

**Page 9**
1. B
2. D
3. A
4. E
5. C

Correct order is Bonnie, Tina, Ben, Harry, and Sam.

**Page 15**
**Across**
1. warranty
5. negotiate
**Down**
2. thrifty
3. redeem
4. rebate

**Page 21**
1. intermediate
2. medieval
3. mediocre
4. media
5. Middle Ages
6. mediate
**MIDDLE**

**Page 27**
Answers will vary.

**Page 33**
**Across**
1. spire
5. facade
**Down**
2. plaza
3. edifice
4. turret

**Page 39**

**PEARS!**

**Page 45**
1. rancid
2. fragrance
3. aromatic
4. stench
5. rotten
**A NOSE**

**Page 51**
1. sturdy
2. infringe
3. fragile
4. fragment
5. infraction
6. fracture
7. break
**SILENCE**

**Page 57**
Answers will vary.

**Page 63**
1. A
2. E
3. D
4. C
5. B

**Page 69**
1. A
2. A
3. B
4. A
5. B

**Page 75**
**Across**
2. tedious
6. append
7. depend
**Down**
1. pending
3. skirmishes
4. suspended
5. pendant

**Page 81**
1. taunt
2. disdain
3. laud
4. acclaim
5. esteem
6. praise
7. dislike
8. admire

**Page 87**
1. E
2. C
3. D
4. B
5. A

**Page 93**
The words that move are:
1. malevolent
2. heroism
3. famous
4. vile
5. distinguished
6. malevolent
7. intrepid

**Page 99**
**Across**
4. saunter
6. stampede
**Down**
1. bound
2. mosey
3. crash
5. run

**Page 105**
The words that move are:
1. irate
2. melancholy
3. buoyant
4. perturbed
5. serene
6. worried
7. buoyant

**Page 111**
1. monarch
2. monologue
3. monopoly
4. monotone
5. monocle
**ALONE**

**Page 117**
1. droll
2. lampoon
3. ponder
4. whimsical
5. plausible

**Page 123**
1. sequential
2. anachronism
3. novel
4. former
5. latter
6. first
7. second

34. **fragrance** — fragrance: a pleasing smell
35. **aromatic** — aromatic: having a very pleasant smell
36. **fracture** — fracture: to break something
37. **fragment** — fragment: a small piece that is broken off
38. **fragile** — fragile: delicate or easily broken
39. **infraction** — infraction: an action that breaks a rule
40. **infringe** — infringe: to overstep a boundary
41. **banter** — banter: to tease someone in a friendly way
42. **indulge** — indulge: to give in to something
43. **relish** — relish: to enjoy something greatly
44. **revel** — revel: to take great satisfaction in something
45. **excursion** — excursion: a short journey
46. **relinquish** — relinquish: to give up control of something
47. **brawl** — brawl: a noisy fight
48. **assail** — assail: to attack someone with words or actions
49. **dispute** — dispute: to argue
50. **skirmish** — skirmish: a small fight
51. **inspired** — inspired: filling people with strong emotion
52. **insipid** — insipid: dull or flat
53. **intriguing** — intriguing: exciting and engaging
54. **provocative** — provocative: intended to get a reaction
55. **tedious** — tedious: boring and unchanging
56. **suspend** — suspend: to delay or stop something
57. **depend** — depend: to rely
58. **pendant** — pendant: an object that hangs
59. **append** — append: to add a part onto something
60. **pending** — pending: when something is still to be decided upon
61. **taunt** — taunt: to tease
62. **disdain** — disdain: to dislike or look down on something
63. **laud** — laud: to praise
64. **acclaim** — acclaim: enthusiastic approval
65. **esteem** — esteem: respect and admiration
66. **tarnish** — tarnish: to become duller and less bright

(Continued on page 129)

# Index